Pepper, Say Please!

WRITTEN AND ILLUSTRATED

BY:

Sumehra Sneha

Good Morning, Pepper! You have finally woken up.

There you are, Pepper. It is time to eat! Where is your breakfast?

Look, your mom has it. Pepper, what should you say?

Pepper, say please!

Yum, yum, Pepper! Now go eat your treat.

After you eat, you need to brush your teeth Pepper, where is your toothbrush?

Look, your brother Peter has it. Pepper, what should you say?

PLEASE...

Pepper, say please!

Now, now, Pepper, go brush your teeth!

After brushing your teeth, you need to get dressed. Where is your hat?

Look, your sister Piper has it. Pepper, what should you say?

PLEASE!

Pepper, say please!

Nice job Pepper. You look your very best!

Now go get your backpack. It's almost time for school! Where is your backpack?

Look, your dad has it. Pepper, what do you say?

Pepper, say please!

PLEASE!!!

Good job, Pepper! You are all ready to go.

YAY!

Now, what do you say Pepper?

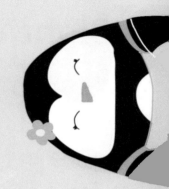

MAY I GO TO SCHOOL, PLEASE?

Of course you can Pepper. Goodbye, and remember to always say please!

Sight Words:

Please
To
Are
Do
Go
You
Up
Has
Yes
Your
Where
There
Is
It
What
Have
For

Extras!

Please, please, please is said,
When you want someone to do
A little something or a favor
That is done for you!

(In the tune of "If You're Happy And You Know It")

If you want a person's favor, what do you say? (Please, Please) *while clapping*
If you want a person's favor, what do you say? (Please, Please) *while clapping*
If you want to be nice and show that you're very, very polite,
If you want a person's favor what do you say? (Please, Please) *while clapping*

(In the tune of "The Wheels on The Bus")

When you need someone's help, you say please,
You say please, you say please.
When you need someone's help you say please,
To everyone.

Can I get on, Please?

Bonus: How to Draw Pepper!

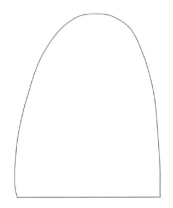

1. Draw a tall igloo.

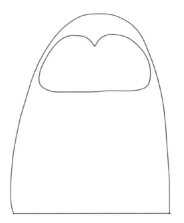

2. Then, draw two bumps, and connect it with a line.

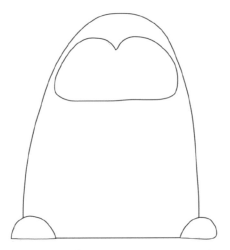

3. Next, draw two oval-like shapes which are flat at the bottom.

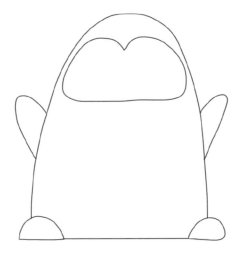

3. Now, draw two long bumps.

Bonus: How to Draw Pepper!

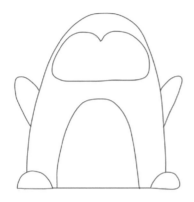

5. Draw another tall igloo.

6. Next, draw two circles, and a triangle.

7. Draw a cap.

8. Color, and now you're done drawing Pepper!

AuthorHouse™
1663 Liberty Drive
Bloomington, IN 47403
www.authorhouse.com
Phone: 833-262-8899

Because of the dynamic nature of the Internet, any web addresses or links contained in this book may have changed
since publication and may no longer be valid. The views expressed in this work are solely those of the author and do
not necessarily reflect the views of the publisher, and the publisher hereby disclaims any responsibility for them.

Any people depicted in stock imagery provided by Getty Images are models,
and such images are being used for illustrative purposes only.
Certain stock imagery © Getty Images.

This book is printed on acid-free paper.

ISBN: 978-1-6655-6584-4 (sc)
ISBN: 978-1-6655-6585-1 (e)

Library of Congress Control Number: 2022913763

Print information available on the last page.

Published by AuthorHouse 08/04/2022

authorHOUSE®

Printed in the United States
by Baker & Taylor Publisher Services